Contents

Page

Preface

Welcome to your Revision Notes.

Your Revision Notes are a summarised version of the material contained in your Course Book. If you find that the Revision Notes refer to material that you do not recollect clearly, you should refer back to the Course Book to refresh your memory.

There is space at the end of each chapter in your Revision Notes where you can enter your own notes for reference.

A note on style

Throughout your Study Packs you will find that we use the masculine form of personal pronouns. This convention is adopted purely for the sake of stylistic convenience – we just don't like saying 'he/she' all the time. Please don't think this reflects any kind of bias or prejudice.

December 2012

CHAPTER 1

Introduction to Sustainability

The background to sustainability

'Sustainability' is the ability of an activity to be maintained at a similar level into the future: taking 'a longer-term view when making decisions, to ensure that meeting our own needs does not compromise the needs of others both today and for future generations' (BSI *Sustainable Procurement Guide,* BIP 2203)

Sustainable development

The Brundtland Commission's 1987 report *Our Common Future* contained a general definition of **sustainable development** which is still widely used: 'Development that meets the needs of the present without compromising the ability of future generations to meet their own needs.'

A three-dimensional (economic-environmental-social) view of sustainability subsequently became widely adopted, and in 1997, the term 'triple bottom line' (TBL) was coined by John Elkington to highlight the need for organisations to measure performance in all three areas. Various frameworks recognise:

- Profit (economic performance), People (social sustainability) and Planet (environmental sustainability)
- Economics, Environment and Equity (social justice)
- Resources (the wise use and management of economic and natural resources) and Respect (for people and other living things).

Economic systems depend on two basic processes: demand and supply. Sustainable development therefore requires the economic, environmental and social sustainability of both consumption (demand-side processes) and production (supply-side processes). 'Sustainable Consumption and Production' (SCP) is a term used to describe this aspect of sustainable development.

Sustainable procurement

The UK Sustainable Procurement Task Force (*Procuring the Future*) defines **sustainable procurement** as: 'A process whereby organisations meet their needs for goods, services, works and utilities in a way that achieves value for money on a whole-life basis in terms of generating benefits not only to the organisation, but also to society and the economy, whilst minimising damage to the environment.'

The BSI *Sustainable Procurement Guide* suggests four main aims for sustainable procurement.

- To minimise negative impacts of goods, works or services across their lifecycle and through the supply chain
- To minimise demand for non-renewable resources
- To ensure that fair contract prices and terms are applied and respected, *at least* meeting minimum ethical, human rights and employment standards
- To promote diversity and equality throughout the supply chain

Aspects of sustainability

Sustainable procurement goes by many different names, according to the aspects prioritised: 'green procurement', 'environmental procurement', 'affirmative procurement', 'responsible procurement', 'socially responsible procurement' – and so on.

Social aspects are gaining prominence in the business-focused literature, particularly because of growing awareness of the reputational risk faced by organisations which ignore issues such as child or enforced labour, and workforce or supplier exploitation in their supply chains.

Corporate social responsibility

The term **corporate social responsibility** is generally used to describe 'the concept whereby companies integrate social and environmental concerns in their business operations and in their interaction with their stakeholders on a voluntary basis' (European Commission).

CIPS recognises ten key CSR issues, which are most relevant to supply chains: environmental responsibility, human rights, equal opportunities, diversity, corporate governance, sustainability, impact on society, ethics and ethical trading, biodiversity, and community involvement.

CSR is a significant driver and enabler of sustainable procurement policies and initiatives in the marketplace as a whole – and within a given organisation.

Environmental purchasing

'Green' or environmental procurement was once seen as a standalone issue, embracing themes such as: resource conservation; climate change mitigation; waste and emissions management; recycling and disposal; 'green' materials specifications; supply chain environmental management standards; and 'green' design and innovation.

However, environmental purchasing is now generally regarded as part of a wider sustainable procurement approach.

Responsible procurement

The term 'responsible procurement' is sometimes used to describe 'procurement practices that combine commercial considerations with social, labour and environmental performance' (Responsible Purchasing Initiative, *Taking the Lead*).

However, terms such as 'responsible procurement' may also be used to refer more specifically to the *social* dimension of sustainability, addressing issues such as labour relations and working conditions, community involvement, social inclusion and diversity, social justice, fair trading, ethical conduct, the responsible use of market power, and human rights – especially in developing country supply markets.

Some key aspects of responsible procurement highlighted by the RPI's *Buying Matters* report are summarised as follows.

ELEMENT	AIM
Good relationships with suppliers	Buyers aim for long-term, stable, trust-based, risk-sharing relationships
Clear, timely communication	Suppliers know the terms of trade which govern the relationship; receive clear communications about buyer expectations; and are able to feed back on their own needs, in a two-way relationship
Sustainable prices and pricing	Prices paid should allow both supplier and buyer to benefit from the relationship and should enable those further along the chain to also benefit from a price which adequately covers the costs of production
Clear lead-times and payments	Suppliers should have clear, consistent and transparent payment terms and a comprehensive order timetable, including when final specification details for the order will be placed and when delivery is expected.
Respect for human and labour rights in the supply chain	Buyers and suppliers understand and work towards minimum human and labour rights standards. Buyers give preference to suppliers who demonstrate improving social and environmental conditions. Buyers manage their own practices to enable suppliers to observe these standards.
Support for small-scale producers and homeworkers	The percentage of products bought from smallholders, homeworkers, democratic co-operatives and disadvantaged areas does not unintentionally change.

An organisation's social procurement responsibilities can extend to all the individuals and communities involved in, or affected by, the operations of its supply chains.

The RPI also emphasises that 'it is up to the purchasing organisation to select and develop the social, labour and environmental standards they expect of their supply base.'

Drivers for sustainability

Elkington (*Cannibals with Forks,* 1999) suggested a number of key drivers for sustainability: values; markets; transparency; lifecycle technology; partnerships; and corporate governance.

Reasons for an increasing focus on sustainability include:

- Values and awareness: growing awareness of the potential negative impacts of international supply chains
- Accountability: political, public and activist pressure for greater corporate responsibility and accountability
- Stakeholder pressures
- Resource scarcity and resulting rising costs
- Financial pressures: need for cost savings eg through improved resource efficiency
- Marketing and competitive pressures
- Risk: growing awareness of the operational, financial and reputational risks of unsustainable business practices
- Government policy, law and regulation
- Frameworks and initiatives (eg codes of practice, certifications and standards)

In addition, a number of **internal factors** may drive – or restrain – the changes required to embed sustainable procurement in a particular organisation: mission, vision and objectives; existing CSR policies; senior management attitudes; performance management mechanisms; risk management processes; and resource availability.

Drivers emerging and changing over time

Senge (*The Necessary Revolution*) argues that organisations subject to the same environmental drivers may respond in different ways, at different paces and with different motives.

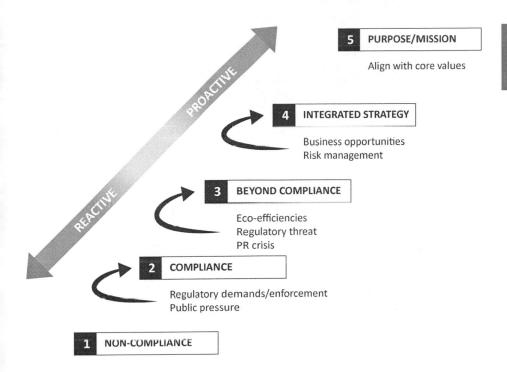

Risks and rewards of sustainability

The business case for sustainability

A number of general **business case arguments** may be advanced for sustainable procurement policies and practices.

Compliance	Law and regulation impose responsibilities on organisations, with reputational, financial and operational penalties for failure to comply
Reputational risk management	Buying organisations are increasingly held responsible for unsustainable behaviour by their suppliers.
Brand development and competitive advantage	Sustainable product design, and sustainably sourced inputs, can create a differentiated brand proposition, which is increasingly valued by consumers.
Workforce and supply base commitment	Above-statutory provisions for the treatment of employees and suppliers may be necessary to attract, retain and motivate quality supply chains
Supply continuity	Support for the financial viability and sustainable practices of suppliers protects the ongoing security of supply.

Continued . . .

Minimisation of failure costs	As in quality management, prevention costs are potentially less than failure costs...
Cost management and efficiency	A focus on whole-life costing approach, resource efficiency and waste reduction can contribute to cost management and profitability.
Improvement and innovation	Sustainable procurement initiatives often require increased supply chain communication, and investment in problem-solving and innovation.
Shareholder value	Companies listed in the Dow Jones Sustainability Group Index (DJSI) have been shown to outperform the general Dow Jones Index over time.

Conflicts and trade-offs in sustainability

In some key areas there will be conflicts, compromises and trade-offs between business objectives and sustainability objectives.

- Social and environmental responsibility may conflict with economic performance (eg through low-cost sourcing).
- Short-term cost is generally perceived as an issue for sustainable procurement.
- Common standards are key enablers of sustainable supply – but by lifting general practice they increase competition and erode competitive advantage.
- Concern for environmental and social issues is a luxury for corporations in less affluent economies and/or economic downturns.
- It is difficult to make a genuine business case for TBL, when the costs of sustainability improvements are tangible – and their value is difficult to measure.

Risks and rewards in sustainability

Taking the Lead identifies the following risk- and reward-based driving forces for sustainable procurement.

- Risk drivers: supply chain complexity and loss of control (need for accountability); failure to deliver (by poorly selected suppliers); increased vulnerability to compliance risk; loss of stakeholder trust
- Reward drivers: competitive advantage (supply chain management as a source of value); internal and external stakeholder commitment; responsible trading relationships.

Developing and implementing sustainable procurement policy

The broad objectives of a sustainable procurement policy may include: supporting and demonstrating commitment to sustainability; promoting sustainability through the supply network; promoting compliance; embedding sustainability factors in purchasing decisions; and defining how procurement will support CSR policies.

A framework for policy development
- *Define the vision* and its fit within corporate sustainability and CSR strategies (if any)
- *Identify and prioritise key issues/topics and core processes*

1

- *Identify and define opportunities for improvement in priority areas*
- *Assess available resources for improvement*
- *Identify key principles*, values and commitments
- *Identify measurable objectives and targets* for achieving improvement in priority areas
- *Identify roles and responsibilities* in the communication, implementation, operation, monitoring and review of the policy
- *Engage in consultation on the draft policy* and *gain authorisation* for a final version
- *Resource the policy*
- *Document, launch, deploy and integrate the policy*
- *Establish processes for ongoing management and review* of the policy's acceptance, implementation, effectiveness and continuing relevance.

Stakeholder consultation and involvement

There is a strong argument for using a multi-disciplinary project team in the development of sustainable procurement policy. Other mechanisms may also be used, such as: briefing and consultation meetings; circulation of draft policy documents; and one-to-one presentation of proposals to key stakeholders.

Procurement will have a particularly important role in consulting with suppliers.

Identifying sustainable priorities

The first step in developing an effective sustainable procurement policy will be to prioritise sustainability issues, supply categories and action areas. This may be done using techniques such as: review of law and standards; audits; spend analysis; supply chain mapping; portfolio analysis; gap analysis; risk and impact assessments; SWOT analysis; and benchmarking.

OWN NOTES

CHAPTER 2

Sustainability Issues in Supply Chains

Globalisation and supply chains

Globalisation is 'the increasing integration of internationally dispersed economic activity' (Boddy). This may involve globalisation of markets, supply, production and/or finance.

A primary focus of responsible purchasing is the *social* issues arising from *globalisation* of supply: in particular, where buyers in developed countries purchase from (or outsource to) suppliers in developing countries. Developed-country buyers have economic power to ameliorate poverty, inequality and poor labour standards in global supply chains – or to perpetuate them.

STEEPLE factors

The STEEPLE model is a popular tool of environmental analysis, which specifies categories under which external factors impacting on organisations can be analysed.

Examples of **drivers for globalisation**, categorised using STEEPLE, include:

- Socio-cultural: convergence of consumer demand; consumer sustainability values
- Technological: improved logistics; ICT-enabled supply chains; technology transfer
- Environmental: resource and commodity location; resource scarcity and non-renewability
- Economic: competition and financial pressures for low-cost sourcing; cost efficiencies of global sourcing; country-specific costs
- Political: international trade promotion; trading blocs and agreements; host government policies encouraging foreign investment
- Legal: less stringent legislative and regulatory regimes; harmonisation of standards
- Ethical: UN and ILO conventions on human and labour rights; support for economic development through international trade

Competitive advantage through global sourcing

The general arguments for and against global sourcing strategies are summarised as follows.

Benefits of global sourcing	Drawbacks of global sourcing
Availability of required materials and/or skills: increased supply capacity and competitiveness	Exchange rate risk and currency management issues etc
Competitive price and cost savings (scale economies, low labour and production costs)	Sourcing and transaction costs (risk management, insurances, tariffs, transport)
Less onerous constraints and costs re environmental and labour compliance	Cost savings and lower standards may create sustainability, compliance or reputational risk
Leverages technology (eg for virtual organisation, e-sourcing)	Different legal frameworks, time zones, standards, language and culture
International trade promotes development, prosperity, international relations etc	Additional risks: political, transport, payment, supplier standards monitoring and so on
Opportunity to develop expertise, contacts and supply networks in potential markets	Environmental impacts of transport and haulage

Global sourcing offers potential for competitive advantage through:

- Cost efficiencies and supply flexibility
- The ability to differentiate the corporate brand
- The ability to attain cost leadership, through lower country-specific costs
- Support for supply chain agility and 'local' supply presence in global markets
- The need to keep pace with globalised competitors.

Globalisation and low cost country sourcing

The key principle of low cost country sourcing is to obtain sourcing efficiencies by identifying and exploiting cost differentials between countries or geographical regions. Brands can produce larger quantities for the same cost, allowing the generation of additional revenue and profits.

Low cost countries may be price-competitive due to: cheap skilled labour costs; abundance of raw materials and resources; low production costs; currency value and exchange rates; favourable taxation regimes; or lack of bargaining power in supply relationships.

Some of these factors pose sustainability issues and risks, with the potential for exploitation of vulnerable suppliers and workers. Some low-cost, developing countries also pose significant business, supply and sustainability risks to buying organisations, and may *not* be an appropriate target for low cost country sourcing.

Overview of sustainability issues

Sustainability issues in globalisation

A number of sustainability-based arguments have been put forward *in favour* of globalisation, eg:

- International trade stimulates local economic activity in developing nations.
- Smaller developing nations benefit from wider markets for their products
- Investment in technology, infrastructure, education and skill development
- Improvements in human rights, labour conditions and environmental management, where foreign investors and buyers operate ethical and CSR policies
- More consumer choice and competitive pricing
- A mechanism for positive international relations.

Those opposed to globalisation argue that it:

- Encourages the exploitation of labour for lower-cost production
- 'Exports' problems of over-consumption and environmental damage
- Encourages unsustainable environmental practices
- Undermines governments in the management of their own domestic economies
- Encourages the exploitation of developing-country markets
- Encourages the homogenisation, commoditisation and erosion of cultures
- Exacerbates unemployment in developed nations
- Disadvantages small and local suppliers in domestic supply markets.

Sustainability issues in supply chains

The following is a summary of economic, social and environmental issues in supply chains, identified by the BSI *(BIP 2203 Sustainable Procurement Guide)*.

ECONOMIC ISSUES	SOCIAL ISSUES	ENVIRONMENTAL ISSUES
Job creation	Creating a diverse base of competitive suppliers	Emissions to air
Achieving value for money	Fair employment practices	Releases to water and land
Supporting SMEs	Promoting workforce welfare	Sustainable use of resources
Reducing barriers to entry (facilitating fair competition)	Supporting skilling and development	Energy and water conservation and management
Ensuring business viability to provide stable employment	Community benefits	Minimisation of waste and by-products
Ensuring supplier agreements are competitive and fair	Fair trade and ethical sourcing practices	Minimisation of impacts

Cultural and social issues

Language and cultural barriers

Cultural barriers may hamper attempts to develop and enforce sustainability standards in cross-cultural supply chains. Examples include cultural and religious norms around gender roles, diversity, consultation and involvement; language differences which may impede the communication and management of standards and policies; assumptions of cultural superiority creating power imbalance in buyer-supplier relations; and cultural differences making externally imposed sustainability solutions impracticable.

Labour standards and forced working

Working conditions may be poor (compared with international standards) in terms of health and safety; the hygiene and amenities of the working environment; hours of work and entitlement to rest breaks; rights of representation; employment security; and adequate pay and benefits.

Suppliers in developing countries may have little or no knowledge of labour laws and standards, and implementation may be weak or absent, due to: lack of resources; lack of political priority; lack of representation and information; and workers not covered (if casually employed).

Wages and social security payments

In the poorest economies, small owners, producers and suppliers may struggle to earn, or pay, a basic living wage. Purchasing organisations may use price leverage to squeeze producers' profit margins – potentially resulting in poverty wages for factory workers, and prices below the cost of production for farmers.

In many developing countries, large numbers of workers lack social security coverage or provision.

Worker inequality

Many people lack access to educational opportunities, basic skills and technological infrastructure and tools that would enable them to aspire to economic participation on more equitable terms.

Access to economic benefits and workforce participation (or 'equal opportunity') varies widely worldwide. A high proportion of vulnerable temporary and part-time workers (who may not be covered by employment laws) are women.

Health and safety standards

Many workers (especially in low-cost countries and vulnerable industries) continue to labour in unsafe working conditions, due to: poor knowledge of standards; lack of compensation regimes; lack of priority and funding; and undeveloped work sites.

What can responsible purchasers do?

Language barriers	• Be sensitive to language issues and use interpretation where appropriate • Check that buyer and supplier share a clear understanding
Cultural differences	• Be prepared to promote and enforce minimum ethical and sustainability standards, regardless of cultural norms • Use understanding, sensitivity and support when communicating, implementing and enforcing standards, expectations and requirements
Labour standards	• Assess whether minimum labour standards are in place • Work with suppliers and worker organisations to better conditions • Consider using a Code of Conduct for suppliers
Wages and benefits	• Pay fair prices which enable suppliers to offer adequate wages • Consider social security provisions when comparing prices
Equality	• Investigate and encourage equal opportunities for women and minorities, where they are under-represented in supervisory and managerial roles • Consider potential risk and exploitation issues for vulnerable groups
Health and safety	• Become knowledgeable about the risks of relevant environments and production processes • Encourage and support suppliers in making effective health and safety commitments and ongoing risk assessments

Environmental issues

Resource consumption

For *non-renewable resources*, the focus is on developing adequate supplies of alternatives. For *renewable resources*, the focus is on: (a) harvesting at a sustainable rate, not exceeding the rate of replenishment, and (b) consuming at a sustainable rate, not exceeding the combined rate of harvest, re-use and recycling of the resource.

Waste management

Waste management focuses on issues such as: reduction of waste materials sent to landfill; increase in the biodegradability of materials; reduction in packaging; design for disassembly, re-use and recycling; reverse logistics capability for take-back and disposal; and compliance with relevant waste management regulations.

Water management

More and more large industrial users of water are beginning to see water supply and management as an area of important business risk and opportunity. In addition, there are pressures on high-risk water polluting industries such as mining, agriculture and manufacturing, to control run-offs, leakage, liquid spills, wastewater discharge and so on.

Climate change

In order to mitigate the effect of human-caused global warming, corporations are urged to reduce greenhouse gas emissions. Procurement-led measures might include: minimising the use of fossil-fuel energy; reducing air freight; carbon offsetting; developing products with a lower carbon impact; sourcing inputs with low carbon impact; and supporting key suppliers and logistics providers in reducing their carbon emissions.

Stakeholder conflicts and trade-offs

The profit motive

The *maximisation* of profit is essentially a 'win-lose' game for the supply chain: the interests of the buyer (forcing supplier prices down) directly conflicts with the interests of suppliers (squeezing margins).

The buyer's profit motive may militate against the interests of suppliers and other stakeholders through: squeezing supplier profit margins; exploiting low-cost labour; opportunistic supplier switching; or seeking cost savings through poor quality, labour or environmental standards.

Demand management and supply flexibility

Supply chain speed and flexibility minimise wastes and inventory costs for the buyer. Urgent and last-minute orders may also arise from buying inefficiencies.

Buyer requirements for speed and flexibility of supply make it difficult for suppliers to estimate and plan adequately to meet demand. Lack of long-term stable supply contracts, low-value short-lead-time orders and/or lack of sharing of accurate demand forecast information are unsustainable where they:

- Pass the risk of demand fluctuations back to vulnerable supply chain members
- Impose unnecessary production, inventory or cancellation costs on suppliers
- Create a disincentive for permanent employment contracts
- Exacerbate the risk of corner-cutting on quality, work conditions and health and safety.

Short-term commercial gains versus long-term security of supply

There may be a trade-off among internal stakeholders between (a) the pressure to make short-term commercial gains and (b) the need to support long-term continuity and security of supply.

Focus on immediate deliverables may jeopardise strategic objectives eg reputation leadership and innovation. Longer perspectives allow stakeholder involvement – supporting waste reduction, innovation, and more committed performance. However, a business case must be made for investing in sustainable supply, on the basis of whole life costs and risk management.

Supplier resistance to buyer-driven sustainability initiatives

Suppliers may themselves resist buyer-driven attempts to improve sustainability standards in the supply chain, due to perceptions of externally imposed pressure to change; costs of developing sustainability; and risk of buyer-specific innovations and adaptations.

OWN NOTES

OWN NOTES

CHAPTER 3

Sustainability Initiatives and Standards

The role of codes and standards

As a minimum, organisations would be expected to comply with – and to purchase from suppliers who comply with – relevant legislation in their own country of operation.

The use of standards, codes of conduct and collaborative initiatives is a way of promoting systematic attention to sustainability issues, and consistent minimum standards of performance.

- **Codes of conduct** specify expected or acceptable ways of behaving.
- **Standards** ('an agreed and repeatable way of doing something', CIPS) specify desired levels of attainment in a particular area of conduct or management.
- **Inspection regimes** (audits) provide assurance that business practices in supply chains are in line with stated CSR policies and standards.

How codes and standards help improve supply chain sustainability

- Allow organisations to demonstrate (give assurance of) their responsibility
- Help manage sustainability risks (eg through supplier pre-qualification and supply chain visibility)
- Provide frameworks and best practice solutions, based on multi-stakeholder input
- Raise stakeholder awareness and supply chain communication on sustainability issues
- Ensure compliance with expected minimum standards
- Encourage the development of sustainability management systems
- Lighten regulatory burdens (through a more flexible and business-oriented approach)
- Provide guidance to facilitate supplier and supply chain development

Issues in the use of supply chain standards

- Implementation is likely to be ineffective without a range of enabling or support activities.
- Codes may be imposed in ways that fail to take supplier constraints into account.
- Standards-related development activities and audits impose costs.
- A focus on auditing and compliance – at the expense of improving performance.
- Multiple codes and audits can cause audit fatigue; supplier confusion; high costs; inefficiency; and focus on compliance at the expense of improvement.

Applying codes and standards effectively

Essential 'complementary enabling activities' include:

- Public and senior management commitment
- Facilitating the building of workers' and suppliers' capacity to improve
- Working with local organisations to raise awareness of labour standards
- Involving suppliers' management and workers in the adoption of codes
- Sharing good practice in the supply chain, industry and multi-stakeholder organisations
- Effective auditing
- Being willing to address purchasing practices which limit improvement
- Recognising and rewarding good performance and improvement

'Ensure: (a) that you know what the standard requires, (b) that this is communicated properly to your suppliers and (c) that they clearly understand the requirements' (BSI).

Labour codes

- Codes for minimum acceptable standards in the employment and mangement of labour are usually based on the 'conventions' or treaties developed by the **International Labour Organisation (ILO)**. It is increasingly common to include Supplier Codes of Conduct based on ILO minimum standards in supply contracts.
- The **Ethical Trading Initiative** (ETI) is a multi-stakeholder association seeking to identify and promote internationally-agreed principles of ethical trade and employment.
- The **Agricultural Ethical Trade Initiative (AETI)** is an example of a multi-stakeholder initiative in an area of trade: agricultural production (vineyards and farms) in South Africa.
- **The SA 8000:2001** standard is a management system standard *and* code of conduct for labour rights, based on ILO conventions in regard to: child labour; forced and compulsory labour; health and safety; freedom of association and right to collective bargaining; discrimination; disciplinary practices; working hours; remuneration; and management systems.

Fair trade standards

The goals of Fair Trade are: to improve the livelihoods and wellbeing of producers; to promote development opportunities for disadvantaged producers; to raise awareness among consumers; to set an example of partnership in trade through dialogue, transparency and respect; to campaign for changes in the rules and practice of international trade.

RESPONSIBILITIES OF SUPPLIERS (PRODUCERS IN DEVELOPING COUNTRIES)	RESPONSIBILITIES OF BUYERS (IMPORTERS IN DEVELOPED COUNTRIES)
• Marginalised, but organised and able to export • Democratic and transparent management • Decent working conditions and a fair wage • Workers have freedom of association • Equal opportunities for all, particularly the most disadvantaged • Long term co-operative relationships • Commitment to invest in the welfare of producers and workers, product quality and environmental stability	• Pay a Fair Trade price (covering costs of sustainable production and living) and a premium to invest in development • Buy from disadvantaged producers • Provide business and financial support (including advance payment where necessary) • Long term co-operative and transparent trading relationships

Fair Trade products are marketed in two different ways:

- Goods are produced, imported and/or distributed by dedicated Fair Trade organisations, under standards developed by the **World Fair Trade Organisation (WFTO)**.
- Fair Trade labelling and certification by an independent third party verification body, to guarantee that production chains respect the International Fair Trade standards developed by **FLO (Fair Trade Labelling Organisations) International.**

FLO International has developed standards mainly covering agricultural products, (a) in formal workplaces (providing for fair wages and a premium fund to benefit workers) and (b) for co-operatives of small-scale producers (providing for a guaranteed minimum price, trading terms based on written contracts, and sufficient lead times).

Environmental management standards

An environmental management system (EMS) is a structured and documented system which manages an organisation's environmental performance.

Relevant standards include:

- ISO 14001: 2004: The Environment Management System Standard
- ISO 14020+: Eco-labelling standards
- The UK Eco-Management and Audit Scheme (EMAS)
- BSI Publicly Available Specification (PAS) 2050: 2011 (assessment of GHG emissions).

Corporate standards and audit systems may be developed by large purchasing organisations.

Codes of practice and standards are also produced by industry associations, particularly for industries which are vulnerable to environmental risks. Examples include the Global GAP (Good Agricultural Practice) standards; the Common Code for the Coffee Community; the Forest Stewardship Council; and the Global e-Sustainability Initiative (GeSI).

General sustainability and sustainable procurement

- The **UN Global Compact** sets out ten principles for business, including: support for human rights (freedom of association and collective bargaining, and elimination of forced and child labour); labour rights; environmental responsibility; and anti-corruption measures.
- **ISO 26000:2010: Guidance for Social Responsibility** provides voluntary guidelines on social responsibility.
- **BS 8903:2010 Sustainable Procurement** is the world's first standard specifically addressing sustainable procurement. Fundamentals (principles) and enablers (supporting factors) are closely aligned to the core themes of the Flexible Framework: the benchmarking framework developed by the UK Sustainable Procurement Taskforce.

The UK sustainable procurement agenda

The **Sustainable Procurement Task Force** presented a National Action Plan (*Procuring the Future,* or the Sims Report) addressing the need for the public sector to: lead by example; rationalise policy; raise the bar; build capacity; remove barriers and stimulate innovation.

Three building blocks for moving the sustainable procurement agenda forward include: prioritisation of spend; the Flexible Framework; and procurement 'tool kits' (including Quick Win minimum sustainable specifications).

The European Commission's **Integrated Product Policy (IPP)** outlines its strategy for reducing the environmental impact caused by products throughout their lifecycle. The IPP is based on five key principles: lifecycle thinking; working with the market; stakeholder involvement; continuous improvement; and policy instruments.

OWN NOTES

3

OWN NOTES

CHAPTER 4

Developing Responsible Procurement

Principles of responsible procurement

'Ten Responsible Procurement Principles' (RPI, *Taking the Lead*):

For senior management

1   Embed responsible procurement in job descriptions and performance reviews
2   Adopt a 'Balanced Scorecard' approach to objectives and rewards

For buyers and buying organisations

3   Make buyers accountable for delivering sustainable standards
4   Build robust sourcing strategy for key categories with complex or high-risk supply chains
5   Subject sourcing strategies to independent review
6   Give suppliers a 'voice'

For supply chains

7   Insist on the use of supply and employment contracts, including sustainability standards.
8   Identify vulnerabilities: apply measures to monitor and manage them.
9   Manage relationships professionally.
10 Encourage collective worker representation

Six 'key success factors' for responsible purchasing: leadership and accountability; knowledge of the consequence of buying actions; managing conflicting priorities; thinking and acting beyond short-term horizons; managing relationships in the supply chain; and responsible use of power in supply chains.

'Six steps to more responsible sourcing' *(Buying Matters)*

1   Understand existing legislation
2   Establish a senior management champion
3   Develop company policies
4   Train buyers
5   Collect data and set benchmarks
6   Assess and reward buyers' and suppliers' performance on responsible purchasing

'Components' of responsible purchasing: good relationships with suppliers; clear, timely communication; sustainable prices and pricing; clear lead times and payments; and respect for human rights in the supply chain.

Implications of responsible procurement

A robust approach to sustainable procurement will have several implications for organisation structure: processes may need to be re-aligned; mechanisms may be required for liaison or cross-functional teamworking; procurement professionals may need to examine and change practices; and there may be operational impacts on other functions in the organisation.

Sectoral differences and issues:

- Private sector organisations are largely driven by competition and the profit motive.
- Public sector organisations are already largely driven by stakeholder needs, social responsibility and sustainability – but constrained by cost drivers.
- The third sector will largely be driven by stakeholder values; reputational risk; stewardship; and cost drivers.

Industry differences and issues:

- Extractive industries face environmental sustainability concerns, social impacts on local communities, and health and safety issues.
- Agriculture has a distinct set of sustainability priorities in regard to the natural environment and supply chain power relationships.
- Manufacturing processes are prone to resource waste, pollution and accidents.
- The focus of the retail sector may be on Fair Trade brands; reduced waste to landfill; ethical supply chain relationships; and end-of-life disposal.

Power in supply chains

Power is essentially exercised in supply chains to appropriate or claim a larger share of the value or value gains created by the process.

French & Raven classified power as: legitimate power; expert power; reward or resource power; referent or personal power; and coercive power.

'Good procurement professionals are aware of the power they exercise and use it responsibly to avoid abuses in the supply chain' (RPI).

The use and leverage of power is a widely used technique, which may: disempower suppliers, creating vulnerability; squeeze supplier profit margins; force suppliers to pursue unsustainable practices; pass risk down the supply chain; discourage supplier input; and stimulate regulatory scrutiny.

Coercive, arbitrary, unfair or abusive exercise of power in supply chains may be seen as a source of sustainability risk.

Responsible use of power in supply chains

Measures that may be taken to improve the responsible use of power by buyers include:

- Training buyers to be aware of their power, and sustainability impacts
- Developing understanding of end-to-end supply chain, and points of vulnerability
- Effective oversight, governance and review of sourcing strategies and supply chains
- Supply chain control, audit and feedback gathering
- Learning from critical incidents and supplier feedback

Power can be *intentionally used to positive effect* in supply chains and supplier relationships: eg to develop suppliers, improve sustainability standards and secure compliance.

Managing conflicting priorities

Responsible purchasing may come under pressure from *internal stakeholders:* eg senior management and in other functions of the organisation. Key challenge of responsible procurement to ensure that:

- Progress in implementing sustainable sourcing practices is not compromised
- The actions and communications of all units and functions of the organisation reflect consistent values and standards.

Value and strategy alignment

Responsible procurement will have to be embedded in the guiding **value system** of the organisation, from the top down.

Vertical and horizontal **alignment** of goals and plans will be required.

Cost barriers to responsible procurement

Sustainable procurement may be more expensive, due to: price premiums for innovation; less scope for opportunistic, price-maximising strategies; higher management costs; development of new capabilities; and significant change management.

Cost barriers may be strengthened by factors such as pressures for short-term profitability; lack of understanding of whole-life costing; and recessionary pressures.

Cost (and cost perception) barriers can be overcome by:

- Selling a longer-term view of cost management (eg whole life costing) to stakeholders.
- Making the business case for sustainability (eg reputational benefits, reduced risk).
- Building momentum, by implementing 'quick wins'
- Offset higher prices by seeking efficiencies elsewhere
- Access financial grants, subsidies, tax breaks and awards.

Sustainability can help *reduce* costs throughout the supply chain, in the long term, eg through: waste reduction, productivity gains, reduced compliance burden, reduced failure costs, and whole-life cost efficiencies.

4

Sustainability risk management

Risk is 'the probability of an unwanted outcome happening' (CIPS). Probability is the measure of the *likelihood* that a given event or result *might* occur.

Lack of sustainability poses risks to an organisation in several key areas.

- **Financial risks** impact on the organisation's ability to trade profitably.
- **Operational risks** (including supply risks) arise from supply chain processes, and impact primarily on production or service delivery.
- **Reputational risks** arise from vulnerability to the exposure of unethical or irresponsible activity by the organisation and/or its supply chain.
- **Compliance and liability risk** arise from exposure of illegal or irresponsible activity by the organisation.

The need for sustainability risk management is highlighted by:

- The transfer of operational management to external enterprises, reducing visibility
- Globalisation, creating lengthier and more complex supply chains
- The consolidation of global buyers, increasing their power over supply markets
- Traditional risk management focusing on risks *to* the business organisation – rather than the risks it poses to vulnerable supply chain resources
- Increasing stakeholder and public awareness of sustainability issues.

Risk management

Risk management involves three key elements: identification, analysis and mitigation.

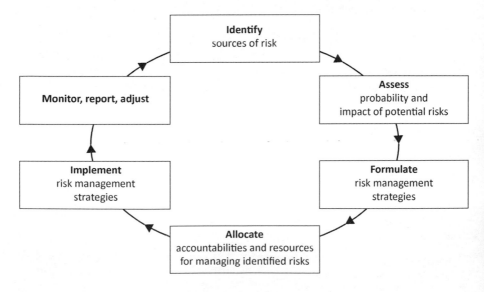

Sustainability through the procurement cycle

The RPI (*Win/Win*) suggests a **responsible purchasing cycle**, with specific reference to purchasing from developing countries. This includes seven stages:

1   Prioritisation of categories and products within the responsible purchasing programme
2   Identification of priority issues in supply chains
3   Supplier market engagement; development of procurement plan
4   Evaluation and shortlisting of suppliers; creation of ITT or RFQ documents
5   Receipt and evaluation of quotes or offers; selection of preferred supplier
6   Creation of contract; and performance management against contract
7   Update responsible purchasing programme and share and reward good practice

OWN NOTES

CHAPTER 5

Sustainable Specification and Contract Development

Identifying and defining requirements

The BSI's *Sustainable Procurement Guide* suggests seven early points for influencing sustainability, before specifications are agreed:

1   Aim to reduce consumption at the start.
2   Develop understanding of business need (and sustainability impacts).
3   Challenge the *status quo*.
4   Understand the power of your spend.
5   Identify positive impacts achievable by your procurement.
6   Consider whole life sustainability issues.
7   Engage the market early.

Identification and definition of requirement is a foundational intervention point for sustainability. Buyers can: challenge customer definitions of requirement; challenge purchase requisitions; ensure that definitions of business need include sustainability requirements; and develop a knowledge bank on sustainable contacts and alternatives.

Developing sustainable specifications

'Capturing sustainability requirements at this point is the *most effective* way of ensuring that sustainability is factored into the purchasing decision.' (BSI *Sustainable Procurement Guide)*

It is common to distinguish between:

*   **Conformance** (or design) specifications
*   **Performance** (functional or outcome) specifications: generally more supportive of sustainability: greater flexibility of supplier base, innovation and problem-solving.

Preferred or desirable specifications may be used to *encourage* suppliers to move towards more sustainable alternatives and to *signal* the importance of improvement – rather than excluding non-compliant suppliers (thereby excluding the potential to make a positive impact).

Key considerations at the need identification and specification stage may be: economic (added value, less waste), social or ethical (labour and human rights standards in the supply chain), and/or environmental (including whole-life impacts).

Social, environmental and economic criteria included in a specification should be shaped by:

- The sustainability objectives of the purchasing organisation
- The key sustainability issues identified in the supply chain and production process
- The points of risk and vulnerability identified through supply chain and portfolio analysis
- The needs and priorities of supply chain stakeholders.

Specifications will often refer to **relevant legislation and standards**, as a kind of 'short-hand' for expressing minimum acceptable process controls and performance levels.

'Quick wins' were developed in the public sector as a set of sustainable specifications for a range of commonly purchased products in each of the priority spend areas. They include mandatory minimum standards plus voluntary best practice specifications.

Developing market knowledge

The purpose of market research, analysis and engagement

For high-value or high-risk procurements, supply market research and/or engagement may be used:

- To ensure that draft specifications have accurately captured sustainability priorities
- To gauge the current level of sustainability capability (and willingness to improve) in the market or supply base
- To identify new sustainable solutions (technologies, products and practices)
- To gauge how much influence the buyer has to drive sustainability (supplier preferencing)
- To identify benchmark levels of sustainability performance in the market
- To promote creativity and innovation, by signaling demand for sustainability, and inviting the early input of potential suppliers to sustainability problem-solving.

Market research and analysis

The RPI recommends supplier market assessment to evaluate:

- The livelihoods and conditions of workers in the supply chain
- Existing national, sectoral or multi-stakeholder initiatives to improve practices
- The level of enforcement of, and compliance with, relevant laws and regulations
- Standards or codes of conduct currently in use.

Similar assessments may be made in relation to environmental issues and impacts.

Market engagement

'Market engagement' means entering into early dialogue with potential suppliers in relation to a given contract or requirement. This may be achieved by issuing a 'draft request' for industry or supply market comment, or by committing to early supplier involvement (ESI).

The main purpose of ESI is to enable a pre-qualified supplier to contribute technical expertise to improve product or service design, or to reduce process costs or wastes.

Benefits of ESI: more accurate and achievable technical specifications; improved product quality and sustainability performance; reduction in development time and costs; better market understanding; and stimulus for partnership relationships and innovation.

Drawbacks of ESI: limitation of design to supplier capability; lock-in to supply relationship; confidentiality and security issues.

Supporting sustainable innovation

If sustainable solutions do not exist yet (or can only be supplied at unacceptably high cost or risk), the buyer may need to (a) establish or signal demand and (b) stimulate innovation.

Sustainable innovation may be defined as 'the successful exploitation of new ideas which further social, environmental or economic sustainability objectives'.

Procurement techniques intended actively to stimulate innovation in the supply chain include:

- Early supplier involvement and partnering
- Supplier development and best-practice sharing
- Innovation councils, or cross-functional innovation steering groups
- Forward Commitment Procurement (FCP): 'a commitment to purchase, at a point in the future, a product that does not yet exist commercially, against a specification that current products do not meet at a sufficient scale, to make it worthwhile for suppliers to invest in tooling up and manufacture' (Sustainable Procurement Taskforce).

Contract negotiation and development

Sustainability considerations will be built into contract and relationship development.

- The sourcing plan (including the type and duration of the supply relationship) will depend on sustainability considerations.
- Responsible purchasers should: provide suppliers with formally agreed, written contracts; insist on written contracts between organisations further down the supply chain; and insist on employment contracts between suppliers and their workers.

Contract negotiation

Negotiation, as an approach to decision-making and influencing, will be important in:

- Securing stakeholder input and buy-in to sustainability policies
- Ensuring that stakeholders' perspectives have been included in decisions affecting them
- Ensuring that contracts reflect genuine agreement between the parties, and a sharing of risk and reward that is broadly acceptable to both parties.

Contract development

Sustainability aspects may be built into the purchase order; standard terms and conditions of purchase; supply contracts; service level agreements; partnership agreements – and any schedules and appendices added to these documents.

The BSI *Sustainable Procurement Guide* offers the following practical guidance.

- Sustainability-related requirements must be clear and non-discriminatory.
- Buyers should generally use standard terms and conditions relating to sustainability.
- Incentives and penalties should be agreed against sustainability and improvement targets.
- Any sustainability commitments or targets agreed in post-tender negotiation should be written into a contract or supplier improvement plan.

Sustainable pricing and payment

The sustainable price for a buyer to pay (purchasing price) will be a price which:

- The purchaser can afford
- Represents value for money for the total package of benefits
- Gives the purchaser a cost or quality advantage over its competitors
- Supports security of supply, and reputational defence, by protecting supplier viability.

The sustainable price for the supplier to charge (sales price) will be a price which:

- 'The market will bear'
- Allows the seller to win business, in competition with other suppliers
- Allows the seller to cover its costs, pay living wages, maintain working conditions and invest in sustainability improvements.

Pricing arrangements

Price arrangements or agreements in contracts are basically of three types:

- **Fixed price agreements**, in which payment is agreed in advance: the supplier bears all the risk of cost variances. Flexible variants (where labour or material costs are volatile), include: contract price adjustment (CPA) clauses; price review clauses; and 'long term stable pricing models'.
- **Incentivised contracts** of various kinds, such as: bonus payments (incentive fees); formulae for sharing cost savings against a negotiated target cost; staged payments; contingency payments; or price penalties for performance failure.
- **Cost-plus agreements**, in which the buyer agrees to reimburse the supplier for all allowable, allocable and reasonable costs incurred in performing the contract, in addition to an agreed profit percentage: the buyer therefore bears the risk of cost variances.

Fixed price agreements may be seen as an unsustainable passing of cost-related risk down the supply chain. Purchasers may prefer to use price review and adjustment provisions within a fixed price arrangement – or cost-plus arrangements.

Cost-plus contracts are often used when long-term quality or sustainability values are more significant to the business need than cost minimisation.

Incentivised contracts may be used to support sustainability by: applying incentives for agreed sustainability improvements; and ensuring that suppliers share equitably in value gains.

Payment terms

Extended payment terms, sale-or-return terms and (non-contracted) late payments, often have significant cashflow implications for vulnerable, cash-or-currency-poor and SME suppliers.

Sustainable payment terms may therefore be based on:

- Pre-payment, payment in advance, or payment with order (in full or deposit)
- Scheduled payments, allowing suppliers to plan cashflows more dependably
- Staged pre-payments (eg on project milestones)
- Self-billing and automatic payments
- Incentives for (or guarantees of) early or prompt payment of supplier invoices

Such terms support sustainability by: giving suppliers assurance of payment; supporting supplier cashflow; giving suppliers revenue assurance (supporting contracted labour and development); and acting as an incentive for sustainability performance.

Other contract terms for sustainability

Community benefits arrangements

A Community Benefits Agreement (CBA) is a formal contract agreed between community groups and a corporation involved in a major supply contract, project or development, requiring the corporation:

- To provide specific amenities, benefits and/or mitigations to the local community
- To consult and negotiate with community representatives on relevant issues, including grievance mechanisms to handle any problems or complaints which may arise.

In exchange, the community groups agree to host, support, or not oppose, the project.

Allowing for lead times and capacity management

Contract provisions may include:

- Forward delivery dates and forecast quantities for large orders
- Guaranteed minimum order quantities where possible
- Achievable lead times between purchase order and delivery (without overtime etc)
- Minimum notice periods for change and/or cancellation of order
- Sharing of information that might impact on purchase schedule or quantity and/or supplier capacity and lead times.

Fair and transparent terms that reward performance

A range of incentives may be used, including:

- Contingency payments (linked to sustainability measures)
- Sustainability KPIs or improvement targets linked to recognition and rewards
- Revenue, profit or gain sharing
- The promise of long-term agreements, increased business, or guaranteed order levels
- The offer of development support.

Statutory compliance

Buyers may use contract terms to 'remind' suppliers of the statutory requirements of relevant law and regulation (eg Health and Safety at Work Act), in order to:

- Signal the importance of compliance with minimum standards
- Clearly apportion liability for compliance-related costs or reputational risks.

OWN NOTES

OWN NOTES

CHAPTER 6

Sustainable Supplier Selection

Sustainability considerations in supplier selection

'Unless robust pre-qualification, tender processes and evaluation criteria are in place to ensure good minimum standards before the supplier is taken on, the purchasing organisation will be constantly undermining its own ethical policies, exposing itself to reputational risk, and giving a signal to the market which undervalues sustainability against other issues.' (BSI)

Sustainability standards may be incorporated at different stages of sourcing eg in:

- Selective request for proposal, quotation or invitation to tender
- Mandatory pre-qualification criteria
- Specifications and statements of requirement
- Qualitative requirements (eg programmes in place or improvement intentions)
- Continuous improvement commitments
- Contract and performance management (KPIs).

Mandatory pre-qualification requirements may limit the number of bids received. This level of conformance may therefore be reserved for procurements for which:

- The organisation needs to address a significant vulnerability
- There are sufficient suppliers willing and able to meet the requirement
- It is permissible (in the public sector) to use selective or restricted tendering procedures.

Qualitative requirements can offer greater flexibility to tender evaluators. They can also be a useful means of promoting consideration of sustainability issues in the supply market, highlighting market demand for sustainability, and stimulating innovative solutions to sustainability problems.

Sustainability-related issues in the selection process itself:

- The process should be fair and transparent, and supportive of fair and open competition
- The process should, as far as possible, engage and support small and diverse suppliers

Supplier pre-qualification

Pre-qualification involves:

- The development of objective **evaluation criteria** by which potential suppliers' sustainability will be screened (and later evaluated in detail)
- The **appraisal and screening** of potential suppliers against stated sustainable procurement objectives.

The starting point may be a pre-qualification questionnaire (PQQ) or request for information (RFI) including sustainability criteria – or a supplier questionnaire specifically focused on sustainability (such as that developed by Oxfam).

Pre-qualification criteria

While the specification typically focuses on the specific nature of the product or service requirement, there is often also a **qualitative requirements** section, focusing on the experience, capacity and service levels of the prospective supplier.

Pre-qualification questionnaires (PQQ)

The aim of a PQQ is to gather information which will enable buyers to assess a supplier's attitude to sustainability; the standards it is currently working to; its current level of sustainability performance; and plans and commitments for future improvements.

When developing pre-qualification questionnaires, buyers should:

- Ensure that information required is proportionate to the importance, risk and complexity of the procurement, and the assessed sustainability risks and impacts
- Pose questions relevant to identified sustainability issues of the procurement category
- Focus on *minimum* standards, so that a range of capable suppliers can proceed to the tender stage.

Appraisal and shortlisting of suppliers

Supplier appraisal for shortlisting may be carried out by: pre-qualification or appraisal questionnaires; perusal of financial statements and reports; checking certifications, accreditations, policy statements and so on; perusal of past audit reports; references from customers, suppliers and relevant NGOs; and checking product samples or portfolios of work.

The buyer may follow up with more labour- and cost-intensive appraisal methods such as a supplier audit, site visit or capability survey for high-risk procurements or supply chains.

Sustainable pre-qualification processes

The process of pre-qualification may in itself be considered a sustainable procurement issue.

- Pre-qualification criteria allow unsuitable suppliers to rule themselves out early – saving them wasted time and cost on bid preparation.
- Prescriptive requirements may unfairly disadvantage some potential suppliers – however, all suppliers can be asked about what steps they are taking to improve sustainability.

- It is good practice formally to notify disqualified suppliers and provide feedback.

Supplier selection

Good practice tender process
- Preparation of detailed specifications and draft contract documents
- Issue of invitations to tender, with specifications (including all sustainability criteria) issued to each potential supplier in identical terms and by the same date.
- Submission of completed tenders or bids by potential suppliers
- Opening of tenders on the appointed date
- Analysis of each tender, according to stated objective criteria
- Tender clarification and verification of supplier information for shortlisted suppliers
- Selection of the best offer, usually on a lowest-price, best value or 'economic advantage' basis. Any non-economic criteria should be clearly notified in the invitation to tender, together with the weightings to be allocated to those criteria.
- Post-tender negotiation, where required and permitted
- Award of the contract and/or establishment of the commercial relationship
- The giving of feedback, on request, to unsuccessful tenderers

Weighted evaluation criteria for supplier selection
Examples of non-cost criteria for supplier appraisal and selection include the following.

ECONOMIC	SOCIAL/ETHICAL	ENVIRONMENTAL
Financial:	*CSR:*	*Environmental impacts:*
• Competitive whole-life cost	• Demonstrated compliance with law and regulation	• Environmental policies
• Financial stability		• Environment management systems (ISO 14001)
• Resource efficiency	• CSR and sustainability policies	
• Cost transparency and fair pricing	• Accreditation to relevant standard (or willingness to work towards standard accreditation)	• Lifecycle impacts of materials, products, packaging and processes
Operational:	• Use of SME and diverse suppliers or subcontractors	• Green design, production and innovation capability
• Production/service capacity		
• Process capability	• Commitment to transparency and improvement	• Transport energy and emissions
• Managerial expertise	*Workforce practices:*	• Reverse logistics, re-use and recycling
• Risk management	• Evidence that workers know their rights and responsibilities at work	
• Supply chain management		• Environmental risk management
Technological:	• Presence of independent trade unions or management-worker committees addressing pay, hours and conditions	• Willingness to 'green'
• Innovation capability		
• Technology leverage	• Monitoring of sub-supplier practices and conditions	
• Compatible information systems	• Participation in multi-stakeholder education and change initiatives	

The overall weighting allocated to sustainability considerations, relative to other criteria (such as technical quality and price) should reflect:

- The contribution of sustainability to the price or value for money assessment
- The significance of sustainability impacts, and scope for improvement
- The potential to influence the market through the procurement.

Receipt and evaluation of tenders

Tenders should be evaluated against the specific, objective award criteria set out in the initial ITT. Normally, the successful tender will be the one with the lowest price, or representing the best economic value over the lifetime of the purchase. However, there may need to be further discussion and analysis among the evaluation team, to decide whether and how effectively each bid meets the requirements.

Site visits or environmental and social audits may be used, once suppliers have been shortlisted at the tender evaluation stage, to gain assurance as to suppliers' conditions, practices and systems. Off-site interviews with workers and ex-workers may also be required, to ensure that they can speak freely.

Recognition of trade unions and collective bargaining arrangements

Individual (non-organised, non-represented) workers are particularly vulnerable to exploitation, especially where they are employed on a temporary or casual basis. The RPI argues that buyers should encourage suppliers to negotiate collective bargaining agreements with independent trade unions on behalf of workers, in order to:

- Help improve and monitor HR practices
- Put in place fair and transparent terms and conditions
- Support supply chain productivity and improvement.

Buyers should gather follow-up information on prospective suppliers' industrial relations, worker representation and rights to collective bargaining, in developing country supply chains.

Purchasing organisations can support sustainable working relationships and conditions, by:

- Giving preference to suppliers who have collective bargaining agreements
- Discussing with preferred suppliers the value of a modern HRM approach
- Promoting 'quick win' improvements, such as appointing health and safety committees
- Taking steps, where necessary, to support 'whistleblowing'
- Signing an international framework agreement with an international trade union.

The use of international framework agreements

International Framework Agreements (IFAs) are generally negotiated between transnational enterprises and Global Union Federations (GUFs) or international trade unions.

IFAs seek to ensure that international labour standards are met in all of a transnational enterprise's locations and supply chains. All IFA agreements are based on the ILO Core Labour Standards.

No legal enforcement mechanisms exist at the global level: enforcement of IFA provisions relies on trade union influence, and management willingness, to resolve complaints.

Contract award

Contracts should be awarded objectively and transparently to the lowest price or best value bid. However, sustainable elements may still be captured in objective and transparent tender evaluation criteria for contract award (BSI).

- Tenders can be risk evaluated (including sustainability risks and impacts) and points awarded to those bids with lower-risk supply.
- Extra points may be awarded for proposals exceeding minimum specified criteria.
- Whole life costing may be used for a more complete picture of the total purchase price.

Whole life costing

Whole life costing enables realistic budgeting over the life of the asset; highlights risks associated with the purchase; promotes cross-functional communication on economic sustainability issues; and supports the optimisation of value for money.

Contract award in the public sector

In the public sector, under the EU Public Procurement Directives, contracts over a certain value threshold must be awarded on the basis of competitive tender, using objective award criteria: lowest price or Most Economically Advantageous Tender (MEAT).

In relation to non-price (eg environmental and social sustainability) criteria:

- Any social or environmental sustainability criteria used must be directly related to the performance of the contract, and appropriately weighted
- Public bodies can specify sustainable options, provided that doing so does not unreasonably distort competition
- EU rules do not permit preference being given to any sector of suppliers, but it is permissible to remove any *obstacles* to competition
- The best opportunity to incorporate sustainability criteria is at specification – and through post-contract negotiated improvement agreements.

Post-tender negotiation

Post-tender negotiation (in the private sector) may offer a good opportunity: to emphasise the need for commitment to sustainability improvement; to check suppliers' understanding of standards; to influence suppliers' sustainability plans; to refine the winning bid in relation to sustainability targets; to mitigate specific risks (eg by agreeing monitoring and reporting measures); or to negotiate into the contract measures that could not be delivered through the tender.

Supplier debrief

Best practice (and public sector tender regulations) dictate that unsuccessful bidders be offered feedback. This supports sustainability by facilitating learning and capability development, and enhancing the ability of small, local and diverse suppliers to compete for contracts.

Supporting SME and diverse suppliers

Small and medium enterprises (SMEs)

There will be a key sourcing trade-off between:

- The economic advantages of dealing with large suppliers (eg through the ability to aggregate requirements for reduced transaction costs and bulk discounts; competitive pricing due to economies of scale)
- The potential for better value in dealing with SME suppliers (eg through more competition; competitive pricing due to lower overheads; innovation capability; expertise in focused niche markets; willingness to produce small-order, customised items; higher levels of service)

Barriers to access for SME suppliers

Barriers to SME participation include:

- Not being able to find out about opportunities
- Lacking marketing resources to raise their profile in the supply market
- Believing that the process involved in bidding will be complex and costly
- Lacking expertise in areas such as constructing tenders
- Lacking a track record of performance for pre-qualification
- Lacking the capacity to handle large volume contracts.

Buyers can support, encourage and facilitate SME participation by measures such as:

- Publicising opportunities widely, particularly for small and low-value contracts
- Using the corporate website to make information available to potential suppliers
- Holding 'Meet the Buyer' events to discuss requirements and sourcing processes
- Ensuring that sourcing procedures are appropriate to size and complexity of requirement
- Keeping tender and specification documents concise and jargon-free
- Using a PQQ to minimise the initial administrative burden on small suppliers
- Setting realistic timescales for sourcing processes
- Considering disaggregating contracts
- Encouraging large first-tier or prime contractors to use SMEs as subcontractors
- Ensuring that the buyer, and its main contractors, pay SME subcontractors on time
- Being open to consortium bids from groups of SMEs, for large procurements.

Supplier diversity and under-represented businesses

Similar considerations may apply in regard to minority-owned and women-owned businesses.

Proactive approaches to improving supplier diversity include:

- Removing barriers to participation in competing for contracts (as for SMEs)
- Positive action policies, whereby suppliers in certain under-represented groups are targeted to offer opportunities to compete for contracts
- Encouraging or requiring suppliers to have diversity plans in place for their supply chains.

6

OWN NOTES

CHAPTER 7

Sustainable Performance Measurement

Sustainability benchmarks and targets

Performance measurement and management

Supplier performance measurement generally implies the comparison of a supplier's current performance against:

- *Defined performance criteria* (such as KPIs or improvement agreements), to establish whether the aimed-for or agreed level of performance has been achieved
- *Previous performance,* to identify deterioration or improvement trends
- *The performance of other organisations* or standard *benchmarks*, to identify areas where performance falls short of best practice or the practice of competitors.

Setting clear goals and targets for sustainable procurement – and then monitoring, measuring, evaluating and reviewing progress and performance – ensures that:

- Deviations or shortfalls can be corrected, and problems identified and solved
- Potential for improvement can be identified and lessons learned for future planning
- Individuals and teams can be motivated by clear objectives, targets and rewards
- Executives responsible to stakeholders can give an accurate account of progress
- The expense of resources can be justified by the results.

Yardsticks for measurement

Performance measures may be formulated as objectives, targets or key performance indicators – which in turn may be formulated as a result of processes such as critical success factor analysis, risk analysis, the use of national or international standards, or benchmarking processes.

Monitoring and measurement

Monitoring methods include self-reporting, audits, inspections or observations, interviews and surveys, and measurements. The focus, criteria and methodology of monitoring may be either quantitative or qualitative.

Performance correction, adjustment and improvement planning

The third phase is the management and adjustment of performance to bring it back 'on course': solving problems, identifying and implementing improvements, and adjusting targets downwards (to be more realistic) or upwards (to set fresh challenges).

Setting sustainability targets and objectives

Influences on supplier performance and improvement targets can be depicted as follows.

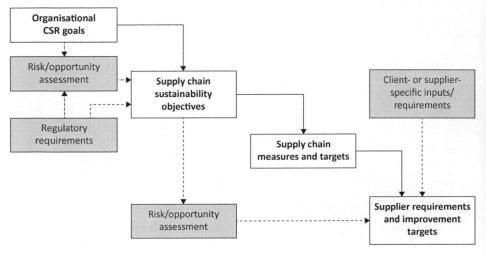

Source: BSI *Sustainable Procurement Guide*

'Not all supplier sustainability requirements may be delivered by the tender and captured in the resulting contract' (BSI). Sustainability requirements may relate to longer-term aspirations and emerging issues. The buying organisation may therefore seek to negotiate improvement targets with suppliers, to be adhered to on a voluntary basis (eg as part of a continuous improvement agreement).

Key performance indicators

Sustainability may be addressed through KPIs by approaches such as:

- Setting specific targets or actions that the supplier is required to attain within a prescribed timeframe
- Requiring a supplier progressively to improve its performance over a given period
- Requiring particular supply chain initiatives
- Requiring suppliers and contractors to provide annual reports on sustainability.

Developing KPIs

'SMART' performance measures are: Specific; Measurable; Attainable; Relevant; and Time-bounded. Some versions of the SMART model substitute or add: Stretching, Sustainable (or Responsible), Agreed and Rewarded.

A simple, generic process for developing KPIs can be summarised as follows.

- Identify critical success factors (CSFs)
- Determine measures of success or improvement for each CSF, working with stakeholders
- Define and agree KPIs with key stakeholders
- Agree monitoring and reporting methods, frequencies and responsibilities.

Advantages and disadvantages of using sustainability KPIs

Benefits of developing KPIs for sustainability:

- Increased (results-focused) communication on sustainability issues
- Motivation to achieve or better the specified performance level
- Support for collaborative buyer-supplier relations
- The ability to identify improvement or deterioration trends
- Focus on key results areas and business risks.

Benefits of KPIs for *supplier* sustainability performance:

- Clear performance criteria and expectations for compliance and improvement
- Supporting contract management and supplier motivation
- Identifying high-performing suppliers for supplier approval and relationship development
- Providing feedback for learning and continuous improvement.

Disadvantages of KPIs: may lead to dysfunctional or sub-optimal behaviour.

Sample KPIs for sustainability

Economic performance:

- *Procurement KPIs* eg cost savings, productivity (eg cost per procurement cycle), supplier leverage, customer satisfaction (eg % OTIF deliveries)
- *Supplier KPIs* eg price, quality and conformance (eg wastage rates), delivery (eg % OTIF deliveries), service relationship, innovation capability

Environmental performance:

- *Procurement KPIs* eg % reduction in energy and water usage; % purchase of recycled materials; volume waste to landfill; % of spend with suppliers who operate an EMS.
- *Supplier KPIs* eg % reduction in GHG emissions; % recycled materials used; progress towards EMS accreditation, attainment of benchmark standards, green innovations

Social and ethical performance:

- *Procurement KPIs* eg diversity of procurement staff; compliance with law and standards; supplier diversity; % suppliers monitored for compliance
- *Supplier KPIs* eg workforce diversity; minimum working conditions and wages; compliance with law and standards; progress towards CSR policy.

Benchmarking

Benchmarking is: 'Measuring your performance against that of best-in-class companies, determining how the best-in-class achieve these performance levels and using the information as a basis for your own company's targets, strategies and implementation' (Pryor).

The Flexible Framework

A key recommendation of the UK Sustainable Procurement National Action Plan: designed to help public sector organisations to review and appraise sustainable procurement capabilities against clear benchmarks, and identify priority areas for improvement.

Five key themes to be addressed	*At five levels of performance*
• People	1: Foundation
• Policy, strategy and communication	2: Embedded
• Procurement process	3: Practice
• Engaging suppliers	4: Enhanced
• Measurement and results	5: Leadership

The balanced scorecard

The Triple Bottom Line accounting

Based on the accounting concept of 'the bottom line' (profit), Elkington's concept of the 'Triple Bottom Line' (TBL, 3BL or People/Profit/Planet) was designed to expand the traditional reporting framework of a company to take into account environmental and social performance (value and costs), in addition to financial performance.

The balanced scorecard

The balanced scorecard (Kaplan and Norton) argues that traditional financial objectives and measures encourage short-termism and are insufficient to control organisations effectively.

Four key perspectives for a balanced scorecard:

- *Financial*. Are we creating value for our shareholders?
- *Customer*. Are we creating value for our customers?
- *Internal business processes*. What are the critical success factors (CSFs) for our business? How efficient and effective are our processes in achieving them?
- *Innovation and organisational learning*. How can we continue to improve and create value?

Incorporating sustainability in scorecards

Some authors have argued that sustainability can be integrated within the balanced scorecard simply by adding a fifth 'sustainability perspective'.

A more integrated approach embeds the balanced scorecard within the 'triple bottom line', with environmental, economic and social objectives for each of the four perspectives.

Blackburn has identified an alternative set of measures built around key stakeholder groups: Employee objectives; Financial (investor/lender) objectives; Supply chain (customer/supplier) objectives; and Citizen (community/government) objectives.

- Employee objectives: build the best global team in our industry
- Financial (investor/lender) objectives: delivering significant shareholder return
- Supply chain (customer/supplier) objectives: create sustainable win-win supply chain relationships
- Citizenship (community/government) objectives: improve lives in local and global communities.

Collaborative performance management

A sustainable supply chain management orientation explicitly recognises the shared responsibility for sustainability. Buyers need to:

- Measure their own performance and practices against sustainability criteria
- Consider the impact of their practices on sustainability further down the supply chain
- Gather feedback from suppliers on the impacts of buying practices
- Consider how strategic suppliers regard them (eg using supplier preferencing).

Performance management itself can be a responsible purchasing issue.

- Overly onerous requirements and targets may be discriminatory
- Overly onerous requirements may lead suppliers to falsify reporting or to cut corners
- Performance measurement may force suppliers into sub-optimal or unsustainable solutions which are ill-adapted to the context and needs of local stakeholders
- Performance appraisals may be *conducted* in an insensitive manner

It is therefore important for the buyer to seek feedback from suppliers as to the impact of the process. Feedback will support relevant and attainable performance measures.

Joint performance appraisal (JPA)

JPA is a relational, collaborative approach to performance measurement, in which the buyer assesses the supplier's performance – *and* vice versa. The objective of this approach is to:

- Recognise the impact of buyer-side processes and behaviours
- Identify problems within the buyer-supplier relationship that may impair performance
- Support long-term value-adding relationships, by ensuring mutual advantage
- Encourage collaboration on continuous, measurable improvements.

The principles of multi-source (360-degree) feedback can be used in JPA.

Complementary buyer/supplier scorecards

The RPI (*Win-Win*) argues that a complementary approach to rewarding good performance (based on an integrated balanced scorecard for buyers and suppliers) recognises the shared responsibility of both parties for sustainability.

Contract and supplier management

Contract management is the process designed to ensure that both parties to a contract meet their obligations, and that the intended outcomes of a contract are delivered. It also involves building and maintaining a good working relationship between the buyer and supplier, continuing through the life of a contract.

Allowing for new developments and targets

New sustainability issues, risks or opportunities may emerge. The buyer may wish to establish commitments and targets for continuous improvement, and related supplier development, within defined planning and review periods (eg year on year).

* Specific year-on-year improvement targets may be agreed at the contract stage
* Alternatively, commitment to continuous improvement may be embedded in the initial contract. Details of moving targets (and the commitment of resources to support them) can then be negotiated and formulated in separate continuous improvement agreements for each planning period.

OWN NOTES

OWN NOTES

CHAPTER 8

Managing Supply Chain Complexity

Supply chain complexity

Supply chain complexity is a key area of vulnerability for sustainable procurement, since:

- In international supply chains, items may be produced, assembled, sold and serviced by suppliers in different countries – often sourced on an opportunistic basis
- The delegation of operational management (eg to tier-one suppliers or outsource providers) reduces transparency and distances the buyer from its supply chain
- Where supply chain complexity increases *and* transparency decreases, the risks are magnified.

The challenge is to monitor, identify and manage sustainability risks 'back' through the tiers of the supply chain. But in complex supply chains, (a) it is not always possible to identify where items 'ultimately' come from and (b) it is costly to monitor and control all tiers and members of the extended supply chain.

Buyers must therefore seek:

- To understand their supply chains, and how complexity creates vulnerability
- To increase the end-to-end visibility of their supply chains
- To identify and prioritise high-risk or high-leverage points in the supply chain.

International supply chains

Internationalised or globalised supply chains add complexity due to a number of factors.

- Physical distance creates (a) logistical complexity and (b) difficulties for supplier appraisal and selection, and sustainability compliance management.
- Legal, cultural and economic differences may create barriers to the management of compliance with standards.

Tiered supply chains

There may be many layers between the top-level purchaser and the 'bottom tiers' of the supply chain, comprising the most vulnerable workers and producers and the most direct environmental impacts. Buyers need:

8

- To improve transparency and support verification of vulnerable supply chains
- To ensure suppliers meet rigorous health and safety, environmental and labour standards
- To implement on-site visits to review standards, for key high-risk contracts
- To work with suppliers and support to help them implement and improve standards
- To support industry-level initiatives, where available.

Subcontracting

The use of subcontractors by suppliers generally adds a layer of complexity and risk, because it creates a situation in which the buying organisation does not have a direct contractual relationship with the contractor, and may not have an opportunity to pre-qualify or approve the subcontractor

Pressure will be put on the buyer to increase the visibility of the supply chain and identify areas of vulnerability.

Supply chain mapping

Supply chain mapping is a tool of analysis and communication, enabling managers to identify:

- Strong and weak linkages in the sustainability chain
- Potential areas of sustainability, compliance or reputational risk
- Potential efficiencies (eg for supply base rationalisation or process alignment)
- Costs, added value, resource usage and environmental impacts at each process stage
- Weaknesses in reverse logistics, or lack of a closed loop supply chain.

Managing for risk and vulnerability

The risk management process

- **Risk identification** is the process of seeking to identify areas of uncertainty: in other words, asking 'what could go wrong?' This may be done by techniques such as: STEEPLE and SWOT; formal risk analysis; critical incident investigations and process audits; consulting with key stakeholders; or employing third-party risk management consultants.
- **Risk assessment or evaluation** is the appraisal of the probability and significance of identified potential risk events: in other words, asking 'how likely is it and how bad could it be?' Quantifying risk allows an organisation to prioritise resources and trigger action.
- **Risk management strategies** ('what can we do about it?') are often classified as the Four Ts: Tolerate (accept); Transfer (spread); Terminate (avoid); or Treat (mitigate).
- **Monitoring, reporting and review** ('What happened and what can we learn?') is important, in order to keep protections effective and up to date.

Portfolio analysis

A key process in sustainabilitiy is the **prioritisation** of areas of procurement, so that efforts can be focused where they have the greatest leverage, impact and return on investment.

The Kraljic matrix

		Complexity of the supply market			
		Low		High	
High	**Procurement focus** Leverage items	**Time horizon** Varied, typically 12-24 months	**Procurement focus** Strategic items	**Time horizon** Up to 10 years; governed by long-term strategic impact (risk and contract mix)	
	Key performance criteria Cost/price and materials flow management	**Items purchased** Mix of commodities and specified materials	**Key performance criteria** Long-term availability	**Items purchased** Scarce and/or high-value materials	
Importance of the item	**Typical sources** Multiple suppliers, chiefly local	**Supply** Abundant	**Typical sources** Established global suppliers	**Supply** Natural scarcity	
	Procurement focus Non-critical items	**Time horizon** Limited: normally 12 months or less	**Procurement focus** Bottleneck items	**Time horizon** Variable, depending on availability vs short-term flexibility trade-offs	
	Key performance criteria Functional efficiency	**Items purchased** Commodities, some specified materials	**Key performance criteria** Cost management and reliable short-term sourcing	**Items purchased** Mainly specified materials	
Low	**Typical sources** Established local suppliers	**Supply** Abundant	**Typical sources** Global, predominantly new suppliers with new technology	**Supply** Production-based scarcity	

Sustainability risk and importance

Some writers argue that the Kraljic matrix: (a) does not sufficiently highlight sustainability risk, and (b) recommends adversarial (potentially irresponsible) procurement approaches.

An alternative approach (RPI) is to map the procurement portfolio on (a) sustainability and compliance risk and (b) its importance to the organisation.

Sustainability risk and scope for improvement

High priority procurements or categories can be *further* classified according to potential **leverage**, or scope for improvement of social or environmental performance (RPI). This approach enables resources to be focused on the risks and impacts where most difference can be made – and hence greater benefits achieved.

Analysis may take into account factors such as: inherent unsustainability; contracts coming up for renewal; actions realistically possible; cost and difficulty of change; and available expertise.

High	**Challenge supplier:** what fundamental changes/ innovations can be made?	**Priority:** Encourage better practices with existing suppliers – or switch to better suppliers
SUSTAINABILITY RISK	**Low priority**	**Quick wins**
Low		

Low — SCOPE FOR IMPROVEMENT — High

Influence and scope for improvement

An added dimension is the extent to which the organisation has *influence to bring about sustainability improvements*. This will take into account the organisation's size and spend, corporate or project profile and status, value as a customer and existing network relationships.

High	Partnership relations with suppliers to: research how to improve	Partnership relations with suppliers to: implement better practices
BUYER INFLUENCE	Encourage suppliers to improve Engage other purchasers to influence sector and supply market	
Low		

Low — SCOPE FOR IMPROVEMENT — High

One factor in assessing influence will be the organisation's value as a customer: the **supplier preferencing model** or supplier attitude matrix.

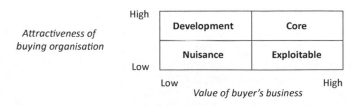

Attractiveness of buying organisation	High	Development	Core
	Low	Nuisance	Exploitable

Low — *Value of buyer's business* — High

Sustainability impact scoring

Buyers need to identify which procurements are likely to have the most significant sustainability impacts, so that mitigating measures can be appropriately targeted.

One simple method is to allocate a **sustainability impact score** to identified high-value, complex procurements, and then to use relative scores to determine priorities. For example:

CRITERION/QUESTION	RATING/SCORE
Does the procurement have a significant environmental or social impact or risk?	**3 High** – significant impact or risk
	2 Medium – some impact or risk
	1 Low – little or no impact or risk

The entire portfolio analyses may be combined and summarised in a **sustainability priority assessment**. For example:

SUSTAINABILITY IMPACT	OPPORTUNITY TO INFLUENCE MARKET	SCOPE TO IMPROVE	PRIORITY	SUSTAINABILITY OBJECTIVE
Energy use	Medium	High	High	Reduce energy consumption during product use

Other tools of analysis

- **SWOT** (strengths, weaknesses, opportunities, threats) analysis is a technique of corporate appraisal, used to assess the *internal* resources of an organisation to cope with and/or capitalise on factors in the *external* environment.
- **Stakeholder mapping** is a tool for categorising and prioritising stakeholders in a project or supply chain, and identifying appropriate strategies to manage them. The most used tool for stakeholder mapping is Mendelow's power/interest matrix.

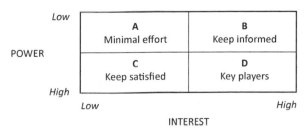

- **Force field analysis** (Kurt Lewin) is a technique for identifying forces for and against change (driving forces and restraining forces), in order to diagnose some of the change management problems that will need to be addressed, and some of the resources and dynamics available to support it.

Supply chain visibility

Managing end-to-end supply chain activity

For many organisations under competitive and recessionary pressure, pursuing ethical monitoring of the supply chain is likely to be seen as an unattainable luxury. However:

- It is possible to **prioritise** items and supply chains for investment in monitoring, on the basis of reputational risk assessment and portfolio analysis.
- Methods of **accessing information** on suppliers are becoming increasingly sophisticated...
- **Experience and expertise** can be accessed eg through third party auditing or risk assessment, and collaboration with multi-stakeholder groups 'on the ground'.

Sustainability impacts also extend *downstream* in the supply chain – all the way to the end users of products and services. The challenge is therefore, increasingly, to manage how products are transported and delivered, advertised, sold, used, returned and/or disposed of. Managing this challenge requires whole-life sustainability planning and downstream partnerships.

Lifecycle management

Whole-life sustainability planning is based on analysis of the sustainability impacts of a product or service over its total life-span.

Supply chain management (SCM)

SCM is: 'The management of upstream and downstream relationships with suppliers and customers to deliver superior customer value at less cost to the supply chain as a whole' (Christopher).

Benefits of an SCM approach to sustainable procurement:

- Eliminating waste and implementing cost reduction through the supply chain
- Integrated responsiveness to sustainability issues and drivers
- Access to complementary resources and capabilities
- Enhanced sustainability performance (eg through collaborative management)
- Faster lead times for product development and delivery
- Better control over performance and risks at lower tiers of the supply chain.

OWN NOTES

8

OWN NOTES

CHAPTER 9

Managing Supply Chain Compliance

Monitoring sustainability performance

Monitoring methods include self-reporting, audits, inspections or observations, interviews and surveys, and measurements.

Difficulties with monitoring in general (Blackburn):

- Qualitative monitoring, being subjective, can lead to doubt and conflict.
- Quantitative measurements are not always easy to make.
- Monitoring systems may not gather or manage information frequently enough.
- Monitoring systems may gather information *too* frequently, creating onerous costs, 'audit fatigue' and information overload.

Supplier performance evaluation or vendor rating

Feedback mechanisms include:

- The gathering of feedback from stakeholders, using interviews and surveys, focus groups, complaint procedures, and project reviews
- The use of observation (eg site visits), testing (eg inspections), and document analysis
- Formal sustainability audits, reviews or vendor rating exercises
- Contract management activities and review meetings
- The use of third-party consultants and auditors.

Sources of sustainability information about suppliers

- Suppliers' published annual reports and accounts
- Suppliers' voluntary sustainability reports
- Sustainability indices, such as the Dow Jones Sustainability Index
- Awards and directories
- The Supplier Ethical Data Exchange (Sedex)
- Public environmental reports posted under the EMAS standard
- Reports posted on the websites of relevant standards organisations and NGOs.

9

Gathering supplier feedback on procurement processes

Identifying indicators and collecting information that highlight 'supplier distress' (eg solvency and liquidity ratios, industrial disputes) might indicate particularly damaging practices.

Feedback should also be sought from suppliers on the impact of sustainable procurement policies and provisions. Such feedback may indicate where requirements are overly onerous or costly to apply, or culturally insensitive.

Subjecting sourcing strategies to independent review

The organisation's sourcing strategies may be subjected to independent review and scrutiny by qualified third parties (such as relevant NGOs or multi-stakeholder organisations).

Supply chain audits

Auditors may be appointed to perform a **systematic review** of an operation, site or function.

'From a sustainable procurement perspective, supply chain audits are used to verify if the supplier organisations are consistently meeting (or are capable of meeting) stated environmental, social and economic requirements'. (BSI)

Types of audit

Types of audit relevant to sustainability monitoring include:

- Compliance audits
- Internal and external standards audits
- A management systems audit (eg ISO 14001 or SA 8000)
- Risk or best practice assessments
- Productivity assessments
- Purchasing management, supplier and supply chain audits
- Environmental (or 'green') audits
- Social audits
- Statutory audits: a legal requirement for corporate governance.

Internal audits are conducted by the organisation's own staff, in the form of self-assessments or independent internal assessments (undertaken by a separate internal auditing group).

External audits are conducted by consultants or other independent entities outside the organisation. This approach is more expensive and potentially disruptive. However, it is useful for adding objectivity, best practice perspectives and credibility.

Supplier audit

Qualified independent auditors will usually be required to conduct supplier certifications under external quality, environmental and social responsibility management standards.

The legitimacy of observation, document-checking and checklist-based approaches to social audits has been challenged, with the increasing recognition that suppliers may seek to 'cover up' human and labour rights abuses. More forensic assessments, including off-site worker interviews, may be required.

Environmental (green) and sustainability audits

Audit tools (Envirowise):

- Audit checklist
- Self-administered questionnaires (to cover matters of fact)
- Interviews (to test staff awareness of issues and policies)
- Discussion (for briefing, consultation and clarification) and
- Reporting on findings, highlighting areas for decision-making and action.

Benefits and drawbacks of the audit approach

Benefits of auditing (Blackburn):

- Providing a new, fresh assessment of gaps in compliance, risk control or efficiency
- Adding credibility to a performance report or business case
- Certifying conformance to an ISO or other recognised standard
- Demonstrating transparency, reducing potential reputational damage.

Drawbacks of auditing:

- The time-consuming and expensive nature of the audit process
- The limitations of audit information
- The risk that auditing itself drives dishonesty (to cover up non-compliance)
- The withdrawal of business from non-compliant suppliers – worsening the situation of vulnerable workers and producers
- The risk of 'analysis paralysis'
- Damage to morale, motivation and relationships
- Over-reliance on auditing, fostering a compliance mentality and a bias for inaction.

Sole reliance on audit data is not advisable: other processes (such as supplier development, and the involvement of trade unions or independent workers' organisations) should be put in place to lead to sustainable improvement in conditions.

Third party auditing

The use of third party auditing services

Feedback on supplier performance may be sought from local organisations or multi-stakeholder coalitions, in order to avoid potential distortion of the facts by suppliers.

The buyer may employ a third-party organisation (eg an NGO or commercial audit company), to provide one-off or periodic supplier auditing services, particularly where:

- The buyer is geographically distant and unfamiliar with the local context
- The buyer wants an independent mandate for corrective action to enforce compliance
- The buyer wants the credibility of third-party assurance for its stakeholders
- Independent third-party audit is a requirement for certification under a standard.

9

Sourcing third-party auditors

Guidelines developed by audit bodies recommend the following general process.

- Determine specific audit requirements
- Identify the attributes and competencies necessary in the auditor (including relevant requirements eg for accreditation)
- Consider (a) a multi-year agreement (b) collaboration with other potential clients
- Establish an audit timetable and work schedule
- Source the market: consult directories; seek recommendations; appraise capabilities
- Communicate requirements and conduct tender or negotiation as appropriate
- Evaluate proposals (criteria eg: adequacy of the proposal; qualifications of staff; size and location of firm; audit protocols used; additional services offered)
- Develop a written contract or engagement letter, documenting expectations.

Assessing the competencies of third-party auditors

Competencies for auditors:

- Demonstrated experience in designing relevant audit programmes
- Detailed awareness of the requirements of standards being verified
- Awareness of relevant issues, industry practices, local customs etc
- Ability to understand relevant company and worker documentation, and its implications
- Interviewing, with particular skills in identifying attempts to hide or falsify data
- Investigative competencies in order to corroborate evidence
- Sensitivity to the need to protect 'whistle blowers'
- Cross-cultural communication competencies
- Team leadership and teamworking competencies, to work in cross-functional audit teams
- Professional integrity
- Well-developed and integrated information systems
- Demonstrated capability in preparing, agreeing and communicating corrective action plans, as the output of the audit process
- Rapid response capabilities, in order to provide audits in the wake of critical incidents
- Willingness to provide integrated audits for multiple clients, to share costs.

Duplication of codes and audits

The proliferation of monitoring systems may result in multiple audits of some suppliers, which can be inefficient and confusing.

Initiatives to promote sharing of audit data: Supplier Data Exchange (Sedex); Achilles Global; E-TASC (Electronics: Tool of Accountable Supply Chains); Global Social Compliance Programme (GSCP); British Socio Compliance Initiative.

Maintaining accountability

Accountability for achieving social, ethical and environmental standards

Responsibility may be allocated to:

- A corporate-level sustainability leader, steering committee or team
- A senior sustainability 'champion' within the procurement function
- The Purchasing Manager, with responsibility to support sustainability policy
- Members of the procurement team, as supervisors, consultants or stakeholder managers.

Sustainability reporting

Reasons for advocating transparency in sustainability reporting:

- Inviting scrutiny – reinforcing accountability
- Highlighting issues and gaps, creating impetus for risk management and improvement
- Encouraging stakeholder communication and education
- Encouraging examples of good practice to emerge
- Building stakeholder trust and organisational resilience
- Ensuring compliance with Business Review requirements, disclosure laws, and EMAS standard requirements for environmental statements etc.

Barriers to sustainability reporting

Reasons why companies do not implement transparent sustainability reporting (Blackburn):

BARRIERS TO REPORTING	WAYS OF OVERCOMING BARRIERS
Embarrassment about performance	Begin with transparency in internal reports
No competitive advantage, if competitors aren't reporting	Draw attention to broad multi-stakeholder support for transparency programmes
Protection of confidentiality	Sell the business case for transparency
Concern about legal liability	Emphasise communicable wins
Concern about negative PR, stakeholder or media responses	Demonstrate resilience of transparent firms: eg Shell, Nike, Johnson & Johnson
Failure to recognise, understand or give priority to the issue	Educate internal stakeholders and demonstrate risks of non-transparency
Belief that cost and effort would be excessive	Reduce costs: start small (scope, frequency), use readily available data and resources, audit internally, combine with other audits

The Global Reporting Initiative

The GRI was started in 1997 with the aim of promoting reporting on economic, environmental and social performance by all organisations. The Sustainability Reporting Guidelines are applicable across sectors and industries, with sector supplements for specific industries and reporting entities.

OWN NOTES

CHAPTER 10

Improving and Developing Compliance

Supplier relationship management

Prioritising relationship investment

A buying organisation may seek to develop closer relationships with suppliers who:

- Offer most potential for capacity-building, ongoing development and added value
- Present a potential risk to the organisation in the area of sustainability
- Require long-term support and development to make sustainability improvements, where this is an important goal of the buyer's supply chain management.

The relationship spectrum

Advantages and disadvantages of collaborative relations for sustainable procurement:

ADVANTAGES	DISADVANTAGES
Greater stability of supply and supply prices	Risk of supplier complacency over time
Greater buyer influence to drive sustainability improvements	Less flexibility to change suppliers at need
Better supplier motivation and responsiveness, arising from mutual commitment and reciprocity	May be locked into relationship with an incompatible, inflexible, under-performing or compliance-vulnerable supplier
Access to supplier's technology and expertise for sustainability	Costs of relationship management and supplier development
Information sharing, supporting capacity planning (which supports labour standards)	Loss of cost gains from opportunistic buying
Ability to plan and collaborate on long-term and continuous improvements	Reputational risk by close association with compliance-vulnerable suppliers

10

Corrective action planning

Gap analysis

Gap analysis involves identifying the difference between the *current* situation or outcomes and *desired* situation or outcomes.

Creating corrective action plans

A corrective action plan (CAP), remediation plan or improvement may be:

- The output of, or response to, an audit process: setting out the specific areas in which improvements or corrections need to be made for compliance with standard
- The output of gap analysis, risk analysis or other problem-identification processes: setting out actions, resources and timescales for resolving the problem or deficiency
- Incorporated in supply contracts and continuous improvement agreements: setting out agreed improvements to be made within the following contract period.

Contents of a corrective action plan or remediation plan:

- A description of each identified infringement or performance shortfall
- The nature of the remedial or corrective action to be taken
- The timescale for the corrective action to be taken
- The persons responsible for implementing the plan
- How compliance with the remediation plan will be monitored, measured and validated
- Any buyer action necessary to support corrective action by the supplier.

Consultation may include purchasers, the owners or managers of the supplier, site managers and worker representatives.

Continuous improvement planning

Sustainability ideally goes beyond mere compliance checking and corrective action planning.

- A 'pass-fail' approach may only perpetuate the problem, if buying organisations withdraw from supply relationships and effectively 'abandon' workers to their fate.
- Compliance auditing may disguise underlying problems, such as lack of information or resources.
- Compliance auditing may actively discourage transparency.

Ideally, sustainable procurement involves:

- The application of progressive, improvement-based standards
- The ongoing examination and improvement of existing processes
- The willingness of both supplier and buyer to collaborate in improvement-seeking
- The active support and investment of the buyer in development and improvement.

Ways of securing continuous improvement:

- Periodically benchmarking performance to identify potential for improvement
- Best-practice sharing

- Gathering feedback from stakeholders
- Implementing rolling performance reviews, objectives and targets
- Negotiating continuous improvement agreements as part of supplier contracts
- Setting up staff and supplier suggestion schemes
- Making progress indicators and reports highly visible.

Raising awareness of standards

Buyers may need:

- To provide suppliers with guidance on good practice and/or standards requirements
- To help suppliers to keep up to date with relevant legislation and industry standards
- To collaborate with local trade unions and other stakeholder advocacy organisations to inform and educate workers about their rights under relevant legislation and standards.

Involving workers in workplace matters

The presence of trade unions or independent workers' organisations on site can help to inform and educate workers about their rights, and to provide formal avenues for workers to discuss issues with management. A buyer may include in its improvement agreement provisions for the establishment of a workers' committee at a supplier factory. Similar arrangements may be made to empower smallholders in dealing with buyers eg through the formation of co-operatives.

Multi-stakeholder collaboration

Collaboration with other stakeholders (including NGOs, industry bodies, other buyers and suppliers) can be useful in continuous improvement initiatives, for:

- Reinforcing the buyer's leverage to drive sustainability improvement
- Harnessing the expertise and networks of organisations dedicated to working within local issues and constraints
- Seeking collective, integrated solutions at a wider level: eg tackling public policy obstacles
- Resourcing supplier development, through guidance, advocacy and consultancy services.

Maintaining commitment to sustainable procurement principles

Strategies for maintaining momentum and commitment:

- Keeping sustainability at 'front of awareness' through ongoing communication
- Maintaining top-level championship
- Implementing rolling reviews and improvement targets, tied to accountabilities
- Implementing periodic learning needs analysis, refresher training etc
- Maintaining risk and environmental reporting, refreshing key issues and drivers
- Setting targets for quick small wins, to create momentum
- Tying continuing improvement to staff and supplier performance appraisals
- Continually documenting and disseminating sustainability results, impacts and benefits

10

Benefits of a continuous improvement approach

- Preventing supplier (and buyer) complacency
- Sustainable change management
- Enabling emerging sustainability issues and priorities to be taken into account
- Co-investment by buyer and supplier in development
- Opportunity for innovation

Supplier development programmes

Hartley & Choi identify two overall objectives for supplier development programmes.

- Raising supplier competence to a specified level (*results-oriented* development)
- Supporting suppliers in self-sustaining required performance standards, through a process of continuous improvement (*process-oriented* development).

Structuring supplier development

Supplier development may involve cross-functional teamwork, or temporary transfers of staff.

Approaches to supplier development

- Enhancing working relationships and procurement practices
- Clarifying performance goals and measures, and associated incentives and penalties
- Seconding buyer staff to the supplier (or *vice versa*) for training, consultancy, liaison etc
- Contributing to the costs of supplier certification
- Providing capital for investment
- Loaning machinery and equipment, or granting supplier access to ICT systems.
- Training supplier staff in relevant areas
- Empowering supplier workers and suppliers to support continuous improvement
- Encouraging supplier forums, consortia and other stakeholder networks

Costs and benefits of supplier development for sustainability

BUYER'S PERSPECTIVE	
COSTS	BENEFITS
Cost of management time in researching, identifying and negotiating opportunities	Improved economic sustainability in the supply chain: reduced supply risk
Cost of development activities: risk of over-investment in a relationship which may not last or prove compatible	Improved sustainability performance by suppliers (and supply chains): reduced sustainability, compliance and reputational risk
Costs of ongoing relationship management (where required)	Streamlining systems and processes: reduced waste, process efficiencies, cost reduction
Risks of sharing information, intellectual property	Support for sustainable outsourcing

Continued . . .

SUPPLIER'S PERSPECTIVE	
COSTS	BENEFITS
Cost of management time in researching, identifying and negotiating opportunities	Support for eco-efficiencies, leading to greater profitability
Risk of over-investment and -dependence, if customer is demanding or unprofitable	Improvements in customer satisfaction, leading to retained or increased business
Costs of ongoing relationship management (where required)	Improved capability for sustainability, leading to additional sales to other customers
Risks of sharing information and intellectual property	Direct gains in knowledge and resources provided by the customer
Cost of discounts or exclusivity agreements given as quid pro quo	Enhanced learning and flexibility: skills for problem-solving and continuous improvement

Customer education and development

One of the key implications of sustainable 'end-to-end' supply chain management is the challenge to educate and develop downstream *customers* as well as suppliers.

Problem-solving and exit arrangements

Managing problems and disputes

Processes to:

- Confront the non-compliant supplier with evidence of infringement
- Confront the non-compliant supplier with consequences of continuing failure to improve
- Diagnose root causes of non-compliance, and collaborate in problem-solving
- Set a time-table for corrective action, with clear consequences for failure.

There may be formal mechanisms for **consultation** and **negotiation** with suppliers to resolve problems or disputes around sustainability compliance.

Handling ETI base code violations

Key principles of handling problems include:

- Transparency
- Co-operative approach
- Respect for the facts
- Direct communication
- Promptness (of investigation and remediation)
- Finality (so that all parties are able to agree that as much as can be done has been done).

10

Escalating problems

Performance agreements will often set out methods to settle infringements of standards, and when and how they will be 'escalated' (taken further or to a higher level) if necessary.

Responsible handling of disputes and grievances

Grievance or dispute mechanisms are structured processes to address problems that arise between two or more parties engaged in contractual or commercial relationships.

- Supply contracts should provide for fair frameworks for mediation or arbitration of contractual disputes.
- Grievance mechanisms may also be used to establish open, transparent and equitable communication channels between business and communities.

Exit arrangements

'Where required improvements have not been made, it may be necessary to exit a relationship with a supplier. This should be a last resort, after the purchasing organisation has made significant effort to support the supplier, but the supplier demonstrates no intention or activity to improve' (RPI).

- There should be a clear understanding of circumstances in which a relationship can be terminated, what processes should be followed, and what notice given.
- Ideally, there should also be provision for review, feedback and learning.
- In a responsible purchasing context, particular consideration will have to be given to the social and economic impacts of termination of contract on dependent suppliers, and their workforces and communities.

OWN NOTES

OWN NOTES